**American Life League's
Life Guide Series**

Volume 1

The Facts of Life

Judie Brown

American Life League, Inc.
Stafford, Virginia

ISBN 1-890712-12-4

American Life League,Inc.
P.O. Box 1350
Stafford, VA 22555

Acknowledgements

This book would not have been possible without the assistance and gentle suggestions of Sheena Talbot, Rebecca Lindstedt, Kate Fitzgerald and Fr. Denis O'Brien, M.M.

Table of Contents

Table of Contents

Natural Law and Moral Principles

"The actions that

we take do affect

others' lives."

Natural Law and Moral Principles

Introduction

What would you think if I told you that this book is going to change the way you look at yourself? Wouldn't it be great to know that there are things about you that are unique and special; that your entire being is a work of nature's art? That's what we are going to learn in these pages.

The Top Ten facts about you

Let's begin with a list of some of the things that make you unique:

- At the moment you were conceived, the information contained in one single strand of your DNA held as much information as 33 volumes of the *Encyclopaedia Britannica*.

- When you were conceived, you were smaller than the dot at the end of this sentence, but you were uniquely and exactly who you are this moment.

- You are the only person in the entire universe who is exactly like you; there are no copies.

- Your entire body and mind—you—are gifts that were given to you by God through your parents.

- You came into this world because no one decided that destroying you by abortion was a better idea than allowing you to be born.

- Your future is dependent in large part on how you welcome and celebrate the lives of others who will be a part of your life as you grow in age and wisdom.

- Your potential to make a significant mark on the world in which you live is limited only by your desire to be the best human being you can.

- Your eyes and ears are the windows of your soul, and through your senses you can learn, absorb and enlighten yourself so that the lessons you have learned in your life can someday help others— maybe your own children!

- You are a unique person in the book of history and are no less important than any other human being in the entire past or future of mankind.

- You are a miracle of tissue, bones, chemicals and more; above all, you can think and you have a free will—the ability to decide what is right and wrong based on absolute moral principles (the Natural Law).

What is meant by absolute moral principles and Natural Law?

Written in the heart (in the conscience) of every man, the Natural Law (absolute moral principles) tells us to do right and to avoid wrong. Man instinctively has the ability to make correct decisions because he has a conscience.

But continual disobedience to this law ultimately blinds the conscience so that we do whatever we wish to do, regardless of the consequences.

Every human being has a conscience. When tough questions are asked, either because of a situation or because of someone else's problems, the individual is challenged to make a decision.

Example #1: A father asks a teenager, "Will you please give up going out Friday night so that Grandma will have company?" The correct answer to this question is, "sure I will!" But the debate that goes on in the young person's mind prior to arriving at the appropriate decision can be pretty difficult.

Sometimes the right decision is not pleasant, but in our hearts we do know what is right—even though it is inconsistent with what our instincts tell us will be the most enjoyable option. This is called an exercise of free will. The decision you make is totally dependent upon your understanding of right and wrong, based on absolute moral principles that do not change.

Example #2: Some people say that no woman should ever be forced to have a baby against her will. Forcing someone to engage in sexual activity is absolutely wrong. Rape and incest are violent crimes. But if, as the result of a violent crime, a woman becomes pregnant, life has now begun for a new individual, separate from his mother's life. There are now three parties in this equation—the woman, the rapist and the child. Obviously, the rapist is guilty and he should be punished. But a child should not be punished because his father committed a crime. At this point, it is best to help the mother see her child as a unique individual with his own Top 10 Facts.

A decision has to made. Unless the problem is examined with a clear understanding of absolute moral principles, the outcome can be tragic, not only for the baby living in the womb, but for his mother and those who advised her.

Example #3: Some people say that they can run around, sleep around and generally do what they please because "nobody is ever affected by what I do." This attitude shows little regard for absolute moral principles. But the attitude is illogical. Many, many people can be affected by our actions.

If someone drinks and drives, the passengers in his car will be affected if he runs the car off the road. If he is driving alone while intoxicated and hits a pedestrian or a second car, many lives are affected immediately. That's why there are laws designed to protect the innocent from the actions of a drunk driver. The drunk driver is behaving immorally and against the law. This driver exercised his free will and made a wrong decision to drink and drive.

If a person is young enough to still be living at home and doesn't arrive home one night at the expected time, parents can be affected emotionally—and sometimes physically. Worry and frustration over not knowing where their child might be or what might have happened can cause anger, anxiety and even physical problems. If the father in this family has a heart condition and stress is not good for him, there could be tragic consequences if his anxiety builds too high.

Parents give children rules when they live at home, and when the children break the rules, the lives of others are affected. When they break these rules they are behaving immorally and against the rules their parents have given them. The young person who is late and does not call has exercised his free will and made a wrong decision.

What if we ignore the laws of man in some other specific way, like shoplifting, for example, and are arrested? Many people would be affected depending on what an individual did to break the law. Again, the person has acted immorally and against the laws of man. The shoplifter has exercised his free will and made a wrong decision.

What if a father of three one day decided not to go home again? What if he didn't call or write or plan to ever let the family know where he was or what he was doing? How many lives would potentially be ruined by this self-centered, "nobody is ever affected by what I do" attitude? Though the police may never find such a father, he has still acted immorally—against the laws that require us to accept responsibility for our actions. This father exercised his free will and made a wrong decision.

We live in a community of human beings. We have family members, friends and others with whom we work or study or play. In each of these cases we are part of their lives and they are part of ours. The actions that we take do affect others' lives. Each of us should be able to think about how we are planning to act, not only to be sure that a particular action is what we want to do and is in agreement with the absolute moral law, but because what we are doing might affect others.

No rational person would ever intentionally want to do anything that might cause another human being to be hurt.

Sometimes, though, we have trouble thinking these things through, and sometimes it seems a lot easier to just go our own way and do our own thing. But it should be clear that the reason there are laws, the reason there are moral ways of behaving, the reason there are times when we cannot do what we want to do because of the way our action might affect others, is to protect ourselves and other innocent human beings who are special and deserve our respect, our love and our time. When we act against the natural law (the absolute moral law) or against the rules set down by human beings, we cause distress, harm and sometimes death.

The same truth about the laws of nature relate to human sexuality. Understanding this will enable you to have a better appreciation of yourself and your fellow human beings.

When you take a few minutes and read the next section, and study the pictures and the graphs, you will begin to see that in the community of man, every human being deserves the right to learn, appreciate and celebrate his Top 10 facts.

Nature and Sexual Intimacy

"Understand the facts

of life and respect the

awesome power . . ."

Nature and Sexual Intimacy

We know that a man and a woman, when joined in sexual intimacy, have the ability, if the man and the woman are fertile, to produce new life. So first let's find out what the word *fertile* means.

Fertile: fruitful, productive, procreative—able to reproduce.

When is a man fertile?

A man usually produces sperm constantly, after he reaches puberty. If he is producing healthy sperm, he is capable of fertilizing a woman's egg with his sperm at any time. A woman's situation is totally different.

When is a woman fertile?

Once a young woman is of reproductive age—usually 12, but the exact age varies—her ovaries begin to release an egg once a month (ovulation). Scientists call this egg an *oocyte*. The woman is aware that this process has begun when she experiences her first menstrual cycle (menses or period). Ovulation causes menses, not the other way around. The beginning of menses is nature's way of letting a young woman know that her body is releasing these eggs each month. There is nothing dirty or unclean about this natural process; it is a normal step in the growth from childhood to adulthood.

A few days before the egg is released, a woman's womb (called the uterus) prepares a nest, making the uterus more hospitable for a possible pregnancy. If a baby is not conceived, the egg dies. The egg leaves her body unnoticed, because it is invisible to the naked eye. The lining of the uterus begins to break down, because it is no longer needed. This process takes about two weeks, and when it is complete the uterine lining leaves the body as menses. Girls should learn to recognize the cervical mucus that indicates the onset and the cessation of ovulation. The program that is designed to help a young woman learn how her body works is called Natural Fertility Awareness.

Now that nature has prepared the way, it is possible for pregnancy to occur.

Some women are infertile, which means their bodies are incapable of producing the healthy eggs needed for fertilization to take place. In most cases, they still have menses, but the eggs their bodies produce are not receptive to the sperm. Infertility is an enormous problem, one that we will discuss later in this book.

Can a woman get pregnant when her period first begins?

Her first periods may be irregular, and the time lapse between them can be as short as 20 days or as long as two months. Very few women have "normal" periods, 28 days apart, especially when the menses have just begun. Women should learn how to observe their cervical mucus every month. Each month is different, and each woman is different. One woman should not compare her cycle with that of any other woman.

Sometimes these periods are painful, and there are even times when ovulation can cause some pain as well, though this is usually slight if noticed at all. If a young woman experiences pain with her period she can seek the advice of a doctor, who can give a complete explanation of this new experience and tell her how she can alleviate the pain that sometimes occurs.

Remember that the egg released in ovulation causes the period. This means that a woman, no matter what her age, can get pregnant if her egg is fertilized by a man's sperm.

What else can you tell me about the egg?

Let's say that a woman has a period and that it lasts from Day one until Day five of a particular month. Typically, she will have ovulated roughly two weeks before the beginning of this period.

She can actually learn how to detect when the egg is present in her fallopian tube by becoming aware of her fertility—a process that is taught very successfully by experts who educate men and women about the principles of fertility awareness.

Remember that the physical maturity of a woman, her body's ability to produce eggs, and the facts surrounding her menses are part of nature's plan. These processes are normal, and the more you can learn about them, the more you will appreciate yourself and your body's capabilities.

If you would like to learn more about fertility awareness, please consult the list of resources at the back of this book to order introductory material, including the names and addresses of teachers in your area who specialize in the subject of fertility awareness. The book *Know Your Body*, listed at the end of this book, also is helpful for parents and young people.

Can pregnancy be avoided if the couple is careful when engaging in sexual activity?

The only way to absolutely avoid pregnancy is to abstain from sexual activity. This is called *practicing abstinence, practicing sexual purity, or remaining chaste*. Only abstinence is risk free. Abstinence is a conscious decision to do without sexual activity. Abstinence is a state of mind and body; it says that you value yourself and others so much that you do not want to do anything that could cause another person grief or stress or a broken heart. It also says that you understand the facts of life and respect the awesome power that nature has given you. Abstinence is your decision to not engage in sexual relations outside of marriage.

On days when the woman is fertile, pregnancy may occur even if there is no entrance of the penis into her vagina and no ejaculation. There is a tiny loss of fluid before full ejaculation, which can cause pregnancy to occur. If you have heard that withdrawal will protect the female from getting pregnant, this is wrong.[1] Sperm can travel in this fluid from the man to the woman.

"Being careful" means practicing abstinence before marriage—period. Any other option, including every type of birth control, is dangerous for you, for the baby you might conceive and for the family you might hope to have later in life.

The Beginning of Life

"**O**nce a fertilized ovum

exists, a new human

being exists."

The Beginning of Life

Is it true that the moment an egg and a sperm actually get together in the woman's body, this action—fertilization—creates a new human being?

That is indeed the truth, though there are many people in our society who will say that the tiny human being who is produced at fertilization is really not a human being. There is a lot of inaccurate information being taught, and it helps to know as much as you can about the facts surrounding the conception of a new human being.

Scientists and philosophers of human embryology, the study of the development of the human being, are called human embryologists. In 1996, one of them, Dr. C. Ward Kischer, Professor of Human Embryology at the University of Arizona College of Medicine, compiled the following list of statements regarding the actual existence of a human being at fertilization. Here is what the experts in the field of human embryology have concluded. While they may occasionally use scientific terms to describe the beginning of life, they share in total agreement that human life does indeed begin at fertilization, when the egg and sperm unite.

Keith L. Moore:

"This fertilized ovum, known as a zygote, is a large diploid cell that is the *beginning, or primordium, of a human being*."

William J. Larsen:

". . . gametes, which will unite at fertilization to initiate the embryonic development of *a new individual*."

Bruce M. Carlson:

"Human *pregnancy* begins with the *fusion* of an egg and a sperm."

Bradley M. Patten:

"[A] fertilized ovum give[s] rise to [a] *new individual*," and "the *process of fertilization* . . . marks the initiation of the *life of a new individual*."

T. W. Sadler:

"The development of a *human being* begins with *fertilization*."

Keith L. Moore and T.V.N. Persaud:

"*Human development* is a *continuous* process that begins when an oocyte (ovum) from a female is *fertilized* by a sperm (spermatozoon) from a male."

Ronan O. O'Rahilly and Fabiola Muller:

"*Fertilization* is an important landmark because, under ordinary circumstances, a *new* genetically *distinct human organism* is thereby formed."

Dr. Kischer reminds us that he has never seen a statement denying the truth of the above. The science is accurate, it is exact, and it is unchanging, regardless of personal opinion or political statements.[2]

A world-famous geneticist, Dr. Jerome Lejeune, the man who discovered the extra chromosome 21 which causes Down Syndrome, once said that "if a fertilized egg is not of itself a full human being, it could not become a man, because something would have to be added to it, and we know that this is impossible." [3]

In summary, to quote Dr. Kischer, it is clear that the union of human sperm and human egg, the fertilized egg:

> is a living entity, a *human being*, a human *individual*, and, a *person*, all one and inseparable. The reason why this is true is: from the moment when the sperm makes contact with the ovum, under conditions we have come to understand and describe as *normal*, all subsequent development to birth of a living newborn is a *fait accompli*. That is to say, after that initial contact of sperm and egg there is no subsequent moment or stage which is held in arbitration or abeyance by the mother, or the embryo or the fetus. Nor is a second contribution, a signal or trigger, needed from the male in order to continue and complete full development to birth. Human development is a *continuum* in which so-called stages overlap and blend one into another.

Indeed, all of life is contained within a time *continuum*. Thus the beginning of a new life is exacted by the beginning of fertilization, the reproductive event which is the *essence* of life.[4]

The new human being, therefore, is completely separate from his mother's and his father's identities after fertilization. No part of the preborn baby is part of his or her mother. Nothing will ever be added during the rest of his life in the womb. The new human being will grow and develop not only in the womb but for his entire life. So when someone argues that the "fetus is just a part of the mother," this is wrong. Yes, the baby is depending on the mother for protection and a place to grow within her, but he is not any more dependent than the newborn who requires protection, care and love.

To quote Sir A. William Liley, this tiny human being "is entirely responsible, not only for his own development, but also for the organization of pregnancy. He has influences, while still no bigger than a grain of sugar, on the mother . . . . While this is by no means novel in biochemical or physiological circumstances . . . it is an astounding feat of power amplification and demonstrates the importance of his own survival to the baby so that he does in fact take over in the human the direct control of the pregnancy." [5]

What does this tiny human being look like?

Look at the drawings on pages 22–23. Look particularly at Step B. You will immediatley notice two things.

The first is that this looks nothing like you do. Go stand in front a mirror and take this book with you. Now look at yourself and then look at Step B. Remember, the drawing is an enlargement—at fertilization, the tiny human being is smaller than the head of a pin and can be seen only with a high-powered microscope.

Look at Step B, and then look at yourself again. At the beginning of your life you looked exactly like Step B!

The second observation is that something amazing takes place in every human being's life during the first six or seven days. Read the description of all that happens in those few days, and realize that the mother and father of this unique human being don't even know yet that he or she is there. Nature is working a miracle within the mother's fallopian tube before she really knows what has happened. Nature is a little like a computer, it produces what you program it to do. But—you can turn off a computer. You can't turn off your body!

Does the DNA molecule present in this new human being change at all during the nine months of pregnancy?

No, it will not change—and cannot change. A DNA molecule is like a very thin thread. It is contained within each of the cells of the 23 chromosomes from the mother and the 23 chromosomes of the father. When these chromosomes unite at fertilization, everything about the new human being is unique, including the DNA, which is unrepeatable ever again—ever!

Figure 1: The Human Embryo—from fertilization until the fifth week after conception

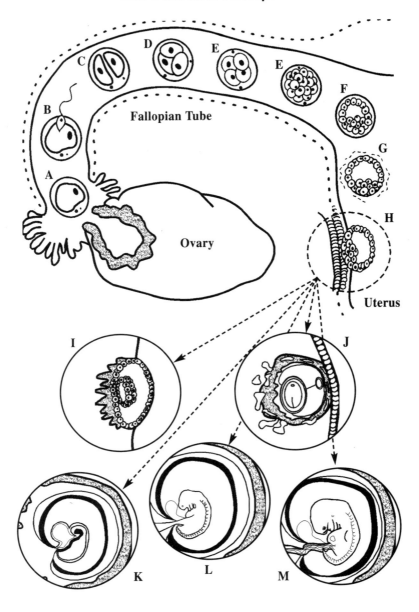

A. Ovulation. The ovum (egg) is released into the Fallopian tube, which is surrounded by a protective covering.[6]

B. Fertilization. A person begins the first day of life within the mother's body. At this point the 23 chromosomes carried by the sperm and the 23 chromosomes carried by the egg combine to form a new one-cell human being, or human embryo, containing 46 chromosomes. The new person is called a human zygote.[7] Each of the 46 chromosomes is composed of genes, or units of DNA, that contain all of the genetic information of the new person.[8] No genetic information is either gained or lost.[9] The zygote is already genetically an individual[10] human being and a "he" or a "she."[11]

C. 24 hours. The zygote divides to form a two-cell embryo.

D. Second day. One of the cells divides. Now the embryo has three cells.

E. Third day. The embryo consists of four cells which divide to make eight, then 16 cells. The 16-cell stage is called the morula stage.[12]

F. Fourth day. Early blastocyst stage. The embryo has entered the uterus.[13]

G. Fifth day. Late blastocyst stage. The outer protective membrane begins to disintegrate as implantation approaches.

H. Implantation of the embryo into the wall of the uterus begins between the sixth and seventh day.

I. Eighth day. Implantation continues.

J. Embryo implantation is complete about day 14. On day 15, the primitive streak (migration of key cells toward the center of the embryo) begins to appear.[14]

K. Third week. The heart begins to beat; neural folds and the major divisions of the brain appear, as well as somites (the neural crest and the beginnings of the internal ear and the eye).[15]

L. Fourth week. The primitive streak begins to disappear. About 30 pairs of somites are present; a large, distinct head and limb buds begin to appear; major outlines of brain and eye vesicles are observable, along with the beginnings of the central nervous system, notochord, mouth and pharynx, body cavity and the basis of the skeleton.[16]

M. Fifth week. The face is taking shape; the forehead, eyes, nostrils and mouth are evident; external ears are beginning; hand and foot plates appear in the limb buds.[17]

The DNA molecule is so tiny that one can hardly imagine not only its size but also the remarkable amount of information it contains. When he testified in the Tennessee frozen embryo case in 1989, Dr. Lejeune discussed the work of a British research scientist, Dr. Jeffreys, who developed a process whereby the DNA molecule can be examined under a microscope. Dr. Lejeune compared the DNA molecule of a human being to the bar code we find on items we purchase in stores:

> Just as the computer at the cash register can read the bar code and provide information for the computer system on the price—the exact identity of the product being purchased, including its color or size—so too can DNA provide an enormous amount of information about a human being. In fact, because of Dr. Jeffreys' discovery, we now know with scientific certainty that there are no two people on this earth who are exactly the same; every human being has his own unique "bar code," and that bar code is present at fertilization.

What exactly does this new human being do for nine months in the womb?

Go back to Figure 1 on page 22. You are going to study a tiny human being who does not look like you but is a person just like you. He's the size of a period at the end of a sentence, but so were you when your life began. Here is a record of life in the womb from fertilization until Month 9:

Fertilization—One little boy begins the first day of his life within his mother's body. At this point his father's sperm and his mother's egg combine to form a new human being who carries with him as much information as the 33-volume *Encyclopaedia Britannica*. This genetic information (DNA) will determine all of this little person's physical characteristics and much of his intelligence and personality.

Day 2—Our little friend is now three cells big. His cells will continue to divide as he begins the journey down his mother's Fallopian tube toward her uterus (womb), where he will get the food and shelter he needs to grow and develop.

Day 6-7—Implantation into his mother's uterus begins and, all the while, he continues to grow. As his cells multiply they differentiate to perform specific functions—circulatory, muscular, neural and skeletal.

Day 14—Implantation is completed around this time, and his mother misses her first menstrual period.

Day 20—His heart, brain, spinal column, and nervous system are almost complete, and his eyes begin to form.

Day 22—His heart begins to beat.

Day 28—This little boy is now approximately one quarter of an inch long—10,000 times larger than he was only three weeks ago! The blood flowing in his veins is completely separate from his mother's.

Week 4—His muscles are developing, and arm and leg buds are visible. His large, distinct head is clearly identifiable along with the major outlines of brain and eye vesicles, the beginnings of his central nervous system, notochord, mouth and pharynx, body cavity, and the basis of his skeleton.

Week 5—Our small friend's face is taking shape; his forehead, eyes, nostrils and mouth are evident; external ears are beginning; hand and foot plates appear in his limb buds.

Week 6—The brainwaves of this little boy can be recorded. His different muscles begin working together.

Week 8—His fingers and toes are fairly well defined, and fingerprints, a unique and defining feature of every human being, are permanently engraved on his skin. All of his organs are present, complete, and functioning (except his lungs). Fifty percent of the abortions performed in America take place between now and Week 9.

Weeks 9-10—All areas of his body are sensitive to touch. He sucks his thumbs, swallows, squints, frowns and puckers his brow. If his palm is stroked, he will make a tight fist.

Weeks 11-12—He now has fingernails, toenails and working taste buds. He can also make all facial expressions, including a smile.

Week 13—Although this baby was already a boy at fertilization, his sex is now identifiable because when we look at the sonogram we can now look for sexual organs.

Month 4—This little baby's heart is pumping six gallons of blood every day, and his mom can now feel him jumping around and turning somersaults, exercising the muscles and lungs he will need to live outside his mother's womb. Rapid eye movement (REM) can be recorded, indicating that he is dreaming.

Months 5-6 —He now weighs about one pound and is a foot long. If he is born now he would have a 50% chance of surviving with the help of dedicated doctors and nurses.

Months 7-8—He can open and close his eyes and recognizes his mom's voice. His weight continues to increase, and "baby fat" fills out and smoothes his skin. If he is born now his chance of surviving increases to 90%.

Month 9—When he is ready to be born he will release hormones to trigger labor. On average he may weigh between seven and nine pounds and can be between 18 and 21 inches long.

Is there any doubt that a new human life begins at fertilization?

None whatsoever. Once a fertilized ovum exists, a new human being exists. There are also special responsibilities that come along with this new person who is, in one sense, totally dependent on his mother even though, in another sense, he is completely independent.

How can the baby living in the womb be independent of his mother?

The mother has a visitor in her womb, and the moment that new human being comes into existence the mother's body is ready to provide for that baby's nurturing. Nature has already worked out the details.

But in a larger sense the baby is the one controlling the situation. Here's what Dr. Lejeune had to say about this (*Tiniest Humans*, p. 68):

Around five days after fecundation [fertilization], this microscopic human being, one millimeter in diameter, sends a chemical message that forces the yellow corpus luteum inside the ovary to produce certain hormones so that the menses of the mother will be suppressed [her period will stop]. It is in fact the baby who suppresses the menses of the mother and who takes over. . . . He is really capable of presiding over his own destiny. Now a little later he will bury himself inside the mucosa [lining] of the uterus and develop a kind of apparatus that I cannot better describe than a cosmonaut's [astronaut's] suit which would have a connection that will have a little cord that will go to the big machine and the big machine would be able to take nutrients from the wall of the uterus through a special respiratory system. And it is the fetus who built this extra thing, this extra surrounding of him, this capsule, and the mother just provides with her blood all the nutrients that can go through the membranes so that the baby can be fed, but the whole machinery, I would say the whole space capsule, is built by the fetus.

This fascinating comparison of the baby in the womb during his first week of life gives you some idea of how amazing this tiny human being already is, how independent he is and how capable he is of setting the tone for the rest of his life in his mother's womb. "There is no question also that in the case of the human fetus this is modifiable by a number of agencies, including external environmental agencies—for instance, a virus infection—and a number of infections that can lead to premature labor. But nevertheless it is the fetus who is physiologically responsible for the triggering of labor." [18]

Because we all know that a picture is worth a thousand words, let's take a look at this little human being, if we could imagine him as the astronaut Dr. Lejeune describes.

From the first moments of his life the baby is in control—that is, unless something happens to harm him. Of course his mother must take care of herself, get proper care and recognize that her own body has special needs as well. But now that she is hosting a visitor, the human being inside knows exactly what must be done as he (or she) prepares for a public appearance at birth.

When will a mother know that she is pregnant?

Modern technology makes it possible for a new mother to know that she is, in fact, a new mother as early as a few days after fertilization occurs. The baby has sent a signal to the mother's body and she will have no more periods until after the child is born. In the meantime, the baby needs sustenance to continue growing and thriving in his mother's womb.

By the time a woman realizes she is a mother, the baby has taken care of business. He has built his "astronaut suit," provided for the life line (umbilical cord) and is well on his way to growing, snugly nestled in his mother's womb.

Making the
Right Choices

"The decision to abort is a criminal act against the laws of nature. It is always wrong."

Making the Right Choices

What am I supposed to do if I want to avoid pregnancy?

The first thing you have to do is remind yourself that you are a valuable human being and that if later in your life you want to become a parent, you will first be married. Between now and that time you will make a commitment to yourself that no one will ever place you in the position of becoming a parent prior to your wedding day.

This decision is often hard, especially for young people. But if you master the ability of thinking about the value of a human being and your own future, it is not impossible. After all, once you become a parent, you are responsible for that baby. Though it is true that many people in our society say they are exercising a "choice" by killing the baby through abortion, the decision to abort is a criminal act against the laws of nature. It is always wrong. Once you admit, with biologists and doctors, that a pregnant woman is a mother of a preborn baby, then the only "choice" is to protect that child.

What if I cannot wait for marriage?

If you think you cannot wait for marriage, think again! You are selling yourself short. You CAN wait! Just think about this. Who will decide your future? Will it be you— or someone who says "everyone's doing it" or who says "If you love me . . . "?

You have grown up in a society that tells you that you are not in control of your desires, that people who abstain from sex until marriage are in the minority, and that you can do whatever you want with your body and give it to whom ever you want as long as you are protected. Such statements are false. You can indeed control your desires. People are finally learning that it is just not worth the emotional and physical risks. The only real form of protection—the only way to avoid pregnancy, AIDS and STD's—is abstinence.

Sexually transmitted diseases sometimes have a side effect that may remain hidden for years. That side effect is often infertility—the inability to have children.

Some women are infertile because their fallopian tubes are blocked for some reason, and they clearly will not be able to become mothers unless a surgical intervention corrects this problem.

But sexually transmitted disease (STD), particularly among unmarried young people, is at epidemic proportions. One of these types of disease is gonorrhea.

Some so-called family planning professionals actually tell people who are diagnosed with gonorrhea that there are no permanent side effects if a couple of pills are taken.

Those professionals are wrong. Many people who have gonorrhea are only partially treated for the disease. They will never be able to have children. They are rendered sterile by the dreadful effects of this disease because gonorrhea, and some other types of sexually transmitted disease, can never be totally cured.

Chlamydia, for example, is another STD that affects many young women. It can be present but not detected until something as dreadful as pelvic inflammatory disease starts. This is a very painful disease, and it too can render women sterile.

It doesn't matter what kind of family planning is suggested. None of them will protect you totally from these dreadful diseases. In fact, some kinds of birth control actually disable the immune system, creating an opportunity for disease to set in.

In 1960 there were only five strains of sexually transmitted disease; in 1996 there were more than 50, including HIV (AIDS) which is incurable—and deadly.

Aren't these statements little more than scare tactics?

Here is a table that was published in the book *Safe Sex* by Joe McIlhaney, M.D. Read it carefully and think about the consequences of not respecting yourself enough to wait for marriage to have sex.

STD

*Then and Now**

Before 1960 **Syphilis and gonorrhea**
The only major STD's.

1976 **Chlamydia** first identified in association with genital infection. A rare disease then, now common.

1981 **HIV** identified. Few cases then. Had killed over 100,000 Americans by the end of 1990.

1984 **Herpes** became common. Doctor office visits for treatment of herpes increased 15-fold between 1966–1984.

1985–1990 **HPV** (human papillomavirus) increased, especially in young people. Example: recent survey revealed 46 percent of sexually active coeds at U.C. (Berkeley) are infected. It is the cause of most cancer of the vulva, vagina, cervix, and penis. Death rate from HPV is about 4800 women annually—more women than are killed by AIDS.

1990 **Syphilis** is at a 40–year high.
Pelvic Inflammatory disease (PID) infects 1 million American women. 16,000 to 20,000 teenagers infected.
Gonorrhea: antibiotic resistant strains present in all 50 states.

*Then: before the sexual revolution of 1960–1990. Now: the result of that sexual revolution.

How do I avoid STD's?

Nature has designed man and woman for exclusive partnerships with one human being in marriage. If men and women recognize the reality of nature's perfect plan, they would never take actions that would violate the natural law and cause themselves, and often others, a lifetime of pain and anguish. STD's don't have to become a part of your life. All you have to do to avoid them is to make a conscious decision to practice abstinence.

What suggestions might help?

Every single person has the ability to control sexual desires. This is easy to do by following a few simple guidelines:

- avoid pornographic material,
- avoid sexually suggestive movies, television shows and magazines,
- avoid situations that might lead to a sexual encounter,
- avoid unchaperoned parties, alcohol and drugs,
- if you live at home, be obedient to your parents,
- state your self-respect up front, no matter who you are with,
- double date,
- dress modestly,
- resolve to save the gift of yourself for your lifetime marriage partner.

It might actually surprise you to find out how many of your acquaintances feel the same way you do but just never mentioned it. By setting a good example for others you could actually help save many of your friends from the difficulties that often result from premarital sex.

Everyone finds certain feelings overwhelming at times. Sexual impulses, for example, can be nearly over-powering, and this is perfectly normal. The question is, will you control those impulses . . .

. . . because you do not want to become a parent at this time in your life?

. . . because you do not wish to spoil the special day when you get married?

. . . because you realize that promiscuity is wrong and you appreciate your own gift of life . . .

or will you allow your impulses to control you?

Moments of intense desire are part of what makes the world go around. The challenge is to choose to be among the people who really want to experience the fullness of living and loving with a special person in the context of marriage. Sex has two natural purposes—love-giving and life-giving. Together these purposes show that sexual intimacy reserved for marriage is good for spouses, their children and society.

What about unmarried people who've already had sexual relations?

Each of us is unique and special—and human. No one is mistake-free. There is no such thing as a human being who has never chosen an avenue in life that turned out to be a dead end, or in some other way lost sight of his goals along the way.

We must never, ever give up on each other, no matter what has gone before us in our lives. There is nothing so bad that it cannot be forgiven. The toughest part about this is usually whether we as human beings are willing to actually forgive ourselves and start all over again.

If you feel that there is something about your life that needs to be corrected, then look in the mirror again and decide that you are just as special as you were the day your life began. But as you are looking, remember too that you are human, which means you are fully capable of making mistakes.

Resolve that you will try again. You may have to try more than once, but the point is—keep trying!

Which important points should I keep in mind?

- Every human being is unique, and life begins at fertilization. There is no other way for life to begin.
- Pregnancy means that two people have become parents to a new human being.
- Avoiding pregnancy means men and women living the virtue of chastity before marriage and fidelity to each other after marriage. Chastity is a way of life that should continue throughout married life because it means that both man and woman are totally—and without question—committed, in marriage, to each other only.
- Avoiding sexually transmitted disease and possible infertility or death means living the virtue of chastity.
- In starting all over again, a person must face his past mistakes, forgive himself and realize that nothing is impossible. We are, after all, unique human beings.

These are the highlights regarding the Facts of Life. If you want to read more about any aspect of what is written here, a complete list of resources appears at the end of this book.

If you want to learn about other life topics, please order one or more of American Life League's *Life Guides*.

Footnotes
and
References

Footnotes

[1] Leonie McSweeney, M.D., *Sex and Conception*, African Universities Press, 1979.

[2] C. Ward Kischer, Ph.D., Affidavit in Support of Doctors for Life of South Africa, 6/7/96.

[3] *The Tiniest Humans/Second Edition,* (Interview with Jerome Lejeune), American Life League, updated 1995, pp. 54–55.

[4] Kischer, op. cit.

[5] *The Tiniest Humans/Second Edition,* (Interview with Sir A. William Liley), American Life League, updated 1995, p. 9.

[6] Bruce M. Carlson, *Human Embryology and Developmental Biology*, Mosby–Year Book, Inc., 1994, p. 23.

[7] Ibid., p. 31; William J. Larsen, *Human Embryology*, Churchill Livingstone, 1993, p. 13. Ronan O'Rahilly and Fabiola Muller, *Human Embryology and Teratology*, New York: Wiley-Liss, 1994, p. 19.

[8] Larsen, op. cit., p. 4.

[9] Alan E. H. Emery, *Elements of Medical Genetics*, New York: Churchill Livingstone, 1983, p. 93. Benjamin Lewin (Ed.), *Genes III*, New York: John Wiley and Sons, 1983, pp. 9–13, 20–203, and 681.

[10] Larsen, op. cit., p. 1; O'Rahilly and Muller, op. cit., p. 20.

[11] Carlson, op. cit., p. 31; Larsen, op. cit., pp. 4–5.

[12] Carlson, op. cit., p. 33.

[13] Carlson, op. cit., p. 44.

[14] Carlson, op. cit., p. 45.

[15] O'Rahilly and Muller, op. cit., p. 35.

[16] O'Rahilly and Muller, op. cit., pp. 60–63.

[17] O'Rahilly and Muller, op. cit., p. 63.

[18] *The Tiniest Humans*, op.cit., p. 15.

References for Further Reading:

The following items are available from American Life League:

The *Life Guide* series:

> *The Facts of Life*
> *The Facts About Birth Control*
> *The Facts About Abortion*
> *Title X: The Six-Billion Dollar Scam*
> *Reflections on Suffering*

The "Answers to Your Questions" series of brochures:

> *Anti-Fertility Vaccines*
> *Condoms and Spermicides*
> *Depo-Provera*
> *Emergency Contraception (The Morning After Pill)*
> *The IUD (Intrauterine Device)*
> *The Medical Abortion (MTX)*
> *The Medical Abortion (RU-486)*
> *Natural Fertility Awareness*
> *Norplant*
> *The Pill*

Know Your Body by Charles W. Norris, M.D., and Jeanne B. Waibel Owen, B.A.

The following publications are also recommended:

Love and Family by Mercedes Wilson, Ignatius Press,

P.O. Box 1339, Ft. Collins, CO 80522, (800) 651-1531

Real Love by Mary Beth Bonnacci, Ignatius Press,
P.O. Box 1339, Ft. Collins, CO 80522, (800) 651-1531

Additional information is available from:

Family of the Americas Foundation
P.O. Box 1170
Dunkirk, MD 20574

Pope Paul VI Institute
6901 Mercy Rd.
Omaha, NE 68106

Appendix A

Appendix A:

Chastity: An Indispensable Virtue
by Ronald Lawler, OFM Cap, PhD

If we wish to be happy, we must learn to be chaste. Chastity is important because chaste love enables us to lay hold of the great human goods which God wants us to obtain through sexuality. And chastity protects us from many tragic sorrows.

St. Thomas Aquinas points out in his *Summa* that sexuality is something important. It lies deep within our being, and it serves basic human goods. Hence it is essential that our sexuality be governed by intelligent love.[1]

Chastity Means Saying YES

Some years ago, with good friends of mine, I wrote a small book called *Catholic Sexual Ethics*.[2] I gave a copy to a priest in the parish in which I was living. He paged through the book gingerly, noting that we actually said that masturbation and contraception were wrong and that fornication and adultery were deeply hurtful, even for consenting adults. "Why," he groaned, "does it take you 276 pages to say NO?"

Somehow he failed to notice that the book was really shouting YES. Chastity, or the wise governance of sexuality, is far from negative. St. Paul once said of Jesus: "For the Son of God, Jesus Christ, was not 'Yes and No';

but in him it is always 'Yes'" (2 Cor. 1:19). And the same can be said of the moral teachings of Jesus: they are a "yes" not a "no." God's precepts do not cramp or narrow our lives. They exclude us from nothing that is rich and good and healing for our lives. God says NO only to NO. That is, he excludes only acts which hurt our own hopes, acts which attack precious good things that our inmost being urges us to love. This double negative is clearly a positive.

We Must Teach Chastity

Though chastity is a virtue human beings naturally need, they often do not realize how much they need it. Parents and other teachers of the faith have to proclaim, and make evident, the goodness of chastity. For we human beings are strangely inclined to pursue every intense pleasure, even when we know that such a pursuit is self-destructive. The fierce cleverness with which the world often urges us to follow the promptings of lust make encouragement toward chastity necessary.

People who have lived chaste lives taste how good and liberating chastity is. And those who have not learned chastity experience how bitter things get when intelligent love does not govern sexuality. Yet they often plead: "Everyone is inclined to enjoy the bright pleasures of sex without careful thinking. This is only natural. We should be free to enjoy sex casually!" But this is a despairing cry. We strange and wonderful human beings are indeed *inclined* often to do stupid things, but we do not need to be pressed into actually *doing* them. Surely we are puzzling creatures: eager to live by intelligent love, and also often moved to serve irrational cravings instead.

Chastity Follows the Pattern of Other Virtues

In other areas of life, those in which we do not become so readily confused as we do in the face of sexual attraction, we know well enough that passionate inclinations often urge us to do things that we know would be stupid and harmful to do. If we have not learned to govern our acts by intelligent love, we are likely to do explosively foolish acts. Goaded by passion, we can destroy a friendship and every manner of good things in our lives.

We know, too, that we are often drawn to enjoy in irresponsible ways the pleasures of eating and drinking. No doubt eating and drinking should be fun. But it is senseless to let the pursuit of pleasure drive us to eat in ways that make us seriously ill or that undermine great human goods like health and energy.

It is just like this with sexuality. We splintered people feel inclined to pursue the pleasures of sex, even in circumstances in which we know it would be self-destructive to do so. But we know that we should let intelligent love master such inclinations. The husband away from home can feel an intense attraction toward sexual activity with someone he does not love, even though he knows that this is quite able to destroy the love between himself and his deeply loved wife. Chastity, like every form of temperance, is not opposed to pleasure. But it enables us to avoid pursuing pleasure in ways that rob us of the good things most dear to our hearts.

Chastity Requires Thinking About Sex

Sometimes it is said that lustful people think too much about sex. This is not true. They may dream about it too much or yield to its charms too foolishly. But what they do not do is think intelligently about sex. Lust does not much care what sex is really for or how one gets possession not only of the shallow and sparkling joys of sex but also of the riches and most enduring goods that it ought to serve.

The chaste person approaches sexuality with thoughtful love. When we are dealing with those enduring goods for which God made sex (personal love, the gladness of unselfish homes, and the blessing of new life) and think about these, we can see for ourselves how wise it is to put off some pleasures for a while. Indeed, we know that those very pleasure can be ours—even more richly—when the approach to sexuality is intelligent.

Our Teaching of Chastity Must be Courageously Counter-Cultural

Many teach our young people about sexuality today. We have Madonna, and Dr. Ruth, and Michael Jackson, and a host of rock stars. It seems that those who have never even tried to grasp what sex is for and whose lives have been bruised by their foolish uses of sex are most eager to teach everybody about sex. Walter Lippman, in his essay "Sex in the Great Society," says that the hucksters of the sexual revolution promised us paradise but led us into the wilderness.[3]

But those who *ought* to be teaching what our sexuality means often do not do so. Many parents and priests and religious educators tell me that they do not really try to teach the Christian vision of sexuality to young people today. "It won't work," they say. But it is far more clear that saying nothing of chastity in a world that drives the young to handle sex disastrously has not been working either. In fact, Christ's vision is the only vision that *does* work to heal our lives.

The Virtue of Chastity Really Works

This sort of counsel is false. When Christ first taught his liberating vision of love and sexuality, he was not living in peaceful times. The Palestine he lived in was an occupied country, and the troops of Rome were not chaste nor did they spread chastity. In a very broken world, Christ taught a sublime sexual ethic, rooted entirely in generous love. He did not look upon the people of his time, wounded as they were by scandalous context of their lives, as incapable of leading great lives. He knew that they were sons and daughters of God and that they were all able, when they were given a right vision and helped by his grace, to lead chaste lives in freedom and love. And he knew that they would not be happy unless they did so.

In the end, the pagan Roman Empire surrendered to Christ's vision of love and the family. One of the chief reasons why pagan Rome became Christian was this: pagan people lived unhappy lives wounded by the lust that their culture taught them was inevitable. They were "free" indeed to do whatever they wished in matters touching sex. But pagan lust led to endless divorce, abortion, infanticide, and hopeless homes. Christian people recognized a duty to take love and the promises of love seriously and to govern their sexual desires by the demands of unselfish love. Intelligent love required them to accept many duties, but they were duties that set them free. The homes of the chaste Christians proved far happier than the homes of the pagans. So the pagans began to long for better things. They too wanted to find wiser patterns of love that heal homes and lives.

In today's world the forces of lust seem far stronger than they really are. But the weakness of lust is that it pursues pleasure foolishly and so loses the precious good things the heart longs for even more than pleasure.

Our world suffers in countless ways from its lust. It will return to wiser ways when it can bear its pain no more, when it comes to realize that the pursuit of pleasure must be intelligent and must care about what is truly good. This return will be hastened if we who have tasted the Christian vision of chaste love learn to teach it gladly and well to those dear to us.

[1] *Summa Theologiae*, II-II, q. 153, a.2,c.

[2] Ronald Lawler, Joseph Boyle, and William E. May, *Catholic Sexual Ethics* (Huntington, Indiana: Our Sunday Visitor, 1985 and 1996).

[3] See Walter Lippman, "Sex in the Great Society," in *The Public Philosophy* (1955).

Reprinted with permission from *The NaProEthics Forum*, Vol. 1, No. 2, November 1996, pgs. 2–3. A subscription to *The NaProEthics Forum* may be obtained by sending $15 to the Center for NaProEthics, Suite 200, 6901 Mercy Rd., Omaha, NE 68106-2604.

Appendix B

Appendix B:

Chastity—Good News for a Love-Hungry Generation

by Mary Beth Bonacci

As a teenager, I was a "nice Catholic girl." And, like all truly nice Catholic girls, I abstained from sexual activity. (For the record, I still do.) My reasons for abstaining as a teen were simple—I didn't want to get pregnant and I didn't want to go to hell.

Good reasons, both. There is nothing quite as compelling as visions of hellfire to counter persistent sexual pressure. Even so, my reasons didn't exactly encompass all of the beauty and wisdom of Catholic Tradition. I don't think it could truly be said that I was practicing the virtue of chastity. I don't think I had even heard the word. (If pressed, I probably would have said that it referred to Sonny and Cher's kid.) For me, abstaining from sex wasn't something positive so much as it was a way of escaping something negative.

That attitude didn't change until my senior year at the University of San Francisco. The St. Ignatius Institute there sponsored a four-part series on chastity. The speakers didn't discuss abstinence. They didn't discuss teen pregnancy or sexually transmitted diseases ("STDs") They discussed the virtue of chastity, in all of its blazing glory. They showed me that chastity—living respect for the incredible gift of human sexuality—is about finding and living real love.

Looking around at my generation, it didn't take a genius to figure out that there was a serious absence of love. It was that need, that hunger for love that was—and still is—driving much of the promiscuity I saw around me. Of course, none of that sexual activity was helping: It was just leading to more problems and more brokenness. Chastity wasn't part of the problem. It was the solution!

That insight changed the course of my life. I decided I wanted to speak on the subject, telling people that chastity is about love. (In 1985, that was a truly radical idea.) Apparently, it was a message the world needed to hear, because the ministry kept growing and, 12 years later, I'm still at it.

Why is chastity about love? To understand that, we need to understand love, not an easy task in this day and age. Love has come to be associated with "feelings" alone, which of course is absurd. Love is more than a feeling. Love is a decision, an act of the will. It means seeing each and every person as made in the image of God, loved by Him, and then treating them accordingly. Love means wanting what is best for the other person, period.

The Language of Human Sexuality

What, then, does sex have to do with love? Sex is an expression of love, yes. But it is an expression of a particular kind of love. Pope John Paul II, in his brilliant "theology of the body," says that sex speaks the language of self-donation. What we do with our bodies, we do with ourselves. In giving their bodies to each other, a man and a woman give themselves to each other. It is a renewal of the marriage sacrament. And, through this act of love, God performs His most creative act: bringing new life into the world. Their married, self-donating love becomes a new image of God with an eternal soul. Love leads to life.

Sex isn't evil. It is good. And it has a logic, a meaning. Sex speaks a language, the language of permanence. Everything about it is oriented to permanent union. Self-donation is permanent. New life is permanent. Our bodies even produce a hormone, oxytocin, in sexual activity. Oxytocin, called "the bonding hormone," causes a strong, enduring emotional attachment between two people. That bond helps married people stay married.

Chastity is simple. It is the virtue which allows us to respect this incredible, powerful gift of human sexuality.

So sex is nice for married people. It bonds them together and gives them children. But that still doesn't answer the larger question: "What does chastity, particularly saving sex for marriage, have to do with finding and living love?"

Unchaste is Unloving

In marriage, sexual union is—and always should be—an expression of love. But what about the unmarried? Can't sex be a loving act for them, too?

Love means wanting what is best for the other. But taking the language of sex outside of the context of marriage is not what is best for the other. It puts the other at risk—physically, emotionally, and spiritually. It uses the "language of the body" in a lie. It abuses the gift of human sexuality. It is not an act of love.

Chastity, then, is freedom to love. For single people, it is the freedom to live their dating years without having to worry about pregnancy, STDs, broken bonds, and sin-induced alienation from God. It is freedom from being used sexually. It is freedom to discern our vocation and, for those who are called to marriage, freedom to find the best possible spouse.

Self-Mastery Is Essential to the Gift

The virtue of chastity is about more than just finding romantic love. Developing the self-control required for chastity is necessary to be able to love in any context.

Sexual expression speaks the language of self-donation. It is a gift of one "self" completely to another. But how can that gift be given freely if the sexual drives are not under control? It is no longer a gift, but rather an irresistible impulse, devoid of any meaning whatsoever.

The sexual drive, like any other human drive, was created by God. It is good. But ever since Adam and Eve, our drives have a tendency to veer off in their own directions. Drives don't know how to love. All they know is "I want what I want when I want it." But it is our will which makes the decision to love, and thus controls the drives.

"Controlling the drives" is certainly easier said than done when it comes to human sexuality. The drives are strong—very strong.

But we cannot, repeat cannot, call ourselves loving people until we have those drives under control (cf. Catechism, nos. 2337 *et seq.*).

Teaching Chastity

The term "chastity" has received a bad rap in the past few generations. It has come to be associated at best merely with abstinence, and at worse with a sort of neo-Manichaean idea that sex is somehow bad or dirty or evil. Many of the teens I speak to have never even heard the word.

Of course, is it any surprise that so few people understand chastity today? When was the last time you saw any literature on this particular virtue? Unless you run in fairly religious circles, the answer may well be "never." In my work, I have been terribly frustrated at the lack of good materials on chastity to supplement my speaking. Much of the literature currently available is "literature rack at the back of the Church" material. Most of it looks like it was written in the 1940's. These pieces often contain good concepts, but their language, design, and presentation are so hopelessly dated that they have virtually zero impact on Catholics of any age today.

Making Chastity Relevant to a New Generation

After 11 years of work in the field of chastity education, I have decided it's time to change all of that. I have formed an organization, Real Love, Inc. Our goal is to provide good, attractive materials that explain and support the virtue of chastity. All of our materials are and will continue to be based on Church teaching, and particularly on Pope John Paul II's theology of the body. We are currently carrying my two books and one video. We soon hope to have developed a brochure series, a study guide, more videos, and a parent program.

The demand for such materials is great. Each radio or television appearance I make on behalf of Real Love, Inc., is followed by a truly overwhelming onslaught of letters and phone calls. Our society has now deprived multiple generations of a true understanding of chastity, and it is obvious to me that its absence is being felt keenly. There is a hunger for information, a hunger for answers to questions which have only been sidestepped for far too many years.

That hunger, of course, is not surprising. Chastity is about love—finding and living real, honest, Christ-like love. The hunger I see is a part of a natural, inborn hunger for love. Without respect and self-control, there can be no love.

In a society with a lot of sex but very little love, chastity is truly good news.

Mary Beth Bonacci is a Catholic speaker and writer, and the founder of Real Love, Inc. She is the author of two books, We're on a Mission from God *and* Real Love, *published by Ignatius Press. For more information on Real Love, Inc., write to 1520 W. Warner Rd., Suite 106–138, Gilbert, AZ 85233.*

Reprinted with permission from *Lay Witness*, Vol. 18, No. 6, July/August 1997, pgs. 6–7. Subscription information may be obtained from Catholics United for the Faith, Inc., International Headquartes, 827 North Fourth Street, Steubenville, OH 43952.

Appendix C

Appendix C:

The Connection Between Contraception and Abortion
by Dr. Janet E. Smith

Many in the pro-life movement are reluctant to make a connection between contraception and abortion. They insist that these are two very different acts—that there is all the difference in the world between contraception, which prevents a life from coming to be and abortion, which takes a life that has already begun.

With some contraceptives there is not only a link with abortion, there is an identity. Some contraceptives are abortifacients; they work by causing early term abortions. The IUD seems to prevent a fertilized egg—a new little human being—from implanting in the uterine wall. The pill does not always stop ovulation but sometimes prevents implantation of the growing embryo. And, of course, the new RU-486 pill works altogether by aborting a new fetus, a new baby. Although some in the pro-life movement occasionally speak out against the contraceptives that are abortifacients most generally steer clear of the issue of contraception.

Contraception creates alleged "need" for abortion

This seems to me to be a mistake. I think that we will not make good progress in creating a society where all new life can be safe, where we truly display a respect for life, where abortion is a terrible memory rather than a terrible reality until we see that there are many significant links between contraception and abortion and that we bravely speak this truth. We need to realize that a society in which contraceptives are widely used is going to have a very difficult time keeping free of abortions since the life-styles and attitudes that contraception fosters create an alleged "need" for abortion.

Planned Parenthood v. *Casey*, the Supreme Court decision that confirmed *Roe* v. *Wade*, stated, "in some critical respects abortion is of the same character as the decision to use contraception . . . for two decades of economic and social developments, people have organized intimate relationships and made choices that define their views of themselves and their places in society, in reliance on the availability of abortion in the event that contraception should fail."

The Supreme Court decision has made completely unnecessary any efforts to "expose" what is really behind the attachment of the modern age to abortion. As the Supreme court candidly states, we *need* abortion so that we can continue our contraceptive lifestyles. It is not because contraceptives are ineffective that a million and a half women a year seek abortions as backups to failed contraceptives. The "intimate relationships" facilitated by contraceptives are what make abortions "necessary." "Intimate" here is a euphemism and a misleading one at that. Here the word "intimate" means "sexual"; it does not mean "loving and close." Abortion is most often the result of sexual relationships in which there is little true intimacy and love, in which there is no room for a baby, the natural consequence of sexual intercourse.

Scholars question overpopulation scare

The Supreme Court, though, is unusually candid. Often, ostensibly more noble reasons are given for the enthusiasm for contraception. For instance, many think contraception crucial for controlling what is perceived to be a great population explosion. But most are unaware that there are very serious scholars who question the legitimacy of the scare of overpopulation in most countries on the earth. Scholars such as Ben Wattenberg, Julian Simon, and Jacqueline Kasun maintain that some countries especially in the west are facing problems of population replacement and that since we are not reproducing our population we will be in for some very hard economic times. These scholars think that much of the problem even in ostensibly overpopulated areas is political and economic rather than demographic—that is, the problem is not one of too many people, but of an improper distribution of goods.

But the topic here is not overpopulation or the merits of contraception as a means to fight overpopulation. Pop-ulation control is not the primary source of the enthusiasm of the modern age for contraception. Rather, contraception currently is hailed as the solution to the problems consequent on the sexual revolution; many believe that better contraceptives and more responsible use of contraceptives will reduce the number of unwanted pregnancies and abortions and will prevent to some extent the spread of sexually transmitted diseases.

To support the argument that more responsible use of contraceptives would reduce the number of abortions, some note that most abortions are performed for "contraceptive purposes." That is, few abortions are had because a woman has been a victim of rape or incest or because a pregnancy would endanger her life, or because she expects to have a handicapped or deformed newborn. Rather, most abortions are had because men and women who do not want a baby are having sexual intercourse and facing pregnancies they did not plan for and do not want. Because their contraceptive failed, or because they failed to use a contraceptive, they then resort to abortion as a backup. Many believe that if we could convince men and women to use contraceptives responsibly we would reduce the number of unwanted pregnancies and thus the number of abortion. Thirty years ago this position might have had some plausibility, but not now. We have lived for about thirty years with a culture permeated with contraceptive use and abortion; no longer can we think that greater access to contraception will reduce the number of abortions. Rather, wherever contraception is more readily available the number of unwanted pregnancies and the number of abortions increases greatly.

Sexual revolution not possible without contraception

The connection between contraception and abortion is primarily this: contraception facilitates the kind of relationships and even the kind of attitudes and moral characters that are likely to lead to abortion. The contraceptive mentality treats sexual intercourse as though it had little natural connection with babies; it thinks of babies as an "accident" of intercourse, as an unwelcome intrusion into a sexual relationship, as a burden. The sexual revolution has no fondness—no room for—the connection between sexual intercourse and babies. The sexual revolution simply was not possible until fairly reliable contraceptives were available.

Far from being a check to the sexual revolution, contraception is the fuel that facilitated the beginning of the sexual revolution and enables it to continue to rage. In the past, many men and women refrained from illicit sexual unions simply because they were not prepared for the responsibilities of parenthood. But once a fairly reliable contraceptive appeared on the scene, this barrier to sex outside the confines of marriage fell. The connection between sex and love also fell quickly; ever since contraception became widely used, there has been much talk of, acceptance of, and practice of casual sex and recreational sex. The deep meaning that is inherent in sexual intercourse has been lost sight of; the willingness to engage in sexual intercourse with another is no longer a result of a deep commitment to another. It no longer bespeaks a willingness to have a child with another and to have all the consequent entanglements with another that babies bring. Contraception helps reduce one's sexual partner to just a sexual object as it renders sexual intercourse to be without any real commitments.

The casualness with which sexual unions are now entered is accompanied by a casualness and carelessness in the use of contraceptives. Studies show that the women having abortions are very knowledgeable about birth control methods; the great majority—eighty per cent—are experienced contraceptors but they display carelessness and indifference in their use of contraception for a variety of reasons. One researcher reports these reasons: she observes that some have broken up with their sexual partners and believe they will no longer need a contraceptive but they find themselves sexually active anyway.[1] Others dislike the physical exam required for the pill, or dislike the side effects of the pill and some are deterred by what inconvenience or difficulty there is in getting contraceptives. Many unmarried women do not like to think of themselves as sexually active; using contraceptives conflicts with self-image. The failure to use birth control is a sign that many women are not comfortable with being sexually active. That is, many of the women are engaged in an activity that, for some reason, they do not wish to admit to themselves.

Frequently, aborted pregnancies are planned

One researcher, Kristin Luker, a pro-abortion social scientist, in a book entitled *Taking Chances: Abortion and the Decision Not to Contracept* attempted to discover why, with contraceptives so widely available, so many women, virtually all knowledgeable about contraception, had unwanted pregnancies and abortions.[2] The conclusions of her studies suggest that it is not simple "carelessness" or "irresponsibility" that lead women to have abortions, but that frequently the pregnancies that are aborted are planned or the result of a calculated risk. She begins by dismissing some of the commonly held views about why women get abortions; she denies that they are usually had by panic-stricken youngsters or that they are had by unmarried women who would otherwise have had illegitimate births. She also maintains that statistics do not show that abortion is an act of final desperation used by poor women and "welfare mothers" or that abortion is often sought by women who have more children than they can handle. What she attempts to discern is what *reason* women had for not using contraception although they were contraceptively experienced and knew the risks involved in not using contraception.[3] Luker seeks to substantiate in her study that "unwanted pregnancy is the end result of an informed decision-making process. That pregnancy occurred anyway, for the women in this study, is because most of them were attempting to achieve more diffuse goals than simply preventing pregnancy." [4]

Luker argues that for these women (who are having non-contracepted sex, but who are not intending to have babies), using contraceptives has certain "costs" and getting pregnant has certain "benefits." The women make a calculation that the benefits of not using contraception and the benefits of a pregnancy outweigh the risks of getting pregnant and the need to have an abortion. She concurs that many women prefer "spontaneous sex" and do not like thinking of themselves as "sexually active." She notes that some wondered whether or not they were fertile and thus did not take contraceptives.[5] The "benefits" of a pregnancy for many women were many; pregnancy proves "that one is a women," [6] or that one is fertile;[7] it provides and excuse for "forcing a definition in the relationship";[8] it forces a woman's or girl's parents to "deal with her";[9] it is used as a "psychological organizing technique."

In the end, almost all of the unmarried women Luker interviewed had the option to marry (and supposedly to complete the pregnancy) but none chose this option. Luker attributes this to unwillingness of women to get married under such conditions, to the disparity between this kind of marriage and their fantasy marriage, and to their belief that they were responsible for the pregnancy, and thus they had no claim on the male's support.[10] One of her examples is of an unmarried woman who did not like using the pill because it made her gain weight. Coupled with this was her wish to force her boyfriend to openly admit his relationship with her to his parents who rejected her, and possibly to force marriage and thus she decided not to use contraception.[11] Upon becoming pregnant, this woman had an abortion.

"Carelessness" is Intentional

Much of this data suggests that there is something deep in our natures that finds the severing of sexual intercourse from love and commitment and babies to be unsatisfactory. As we have seen, women are careless in their use of contraceptives for a variety of reasons, but one reason for their careless use of contraceptives is precisely their desire to engage in meaningful sexual activity rather than in meaningless sexual activity. They want their sexual acts to be more meaningful than a handshake or a meal shared. They are profoundly uncomfortable with using contraceptives for what they do to their bodies and for what they do to their relationships. Often, they desire to have a more committed relationship with the male with whom they are involved; they get pregnant to test his love and commitment. But since the relationship has not been made permanent, since no vows have been taken, they are profoundly ambivalent about any pregnancy that might occur. They are very likely to abort a pregnancy they may even have desired. It may sound farfetched to claim that some women may in some sense "plan" or "desire" the very pregnancies that they abort but this analysis is borne out by studies done by pro-abortion sociologists.

Why do women engage in such self-destructive behavior? Again, a large part of the reason is the incredible emphasis the modern age places on freedom—not on the true freedom we all desire, the freedom to be able to pursue what is good and true, but on a kind of freedom that more closely resembles license—the freedom to do whatever one wants, regardless of what is good and true. We want to be free not to *discover* what is good and true, but to be free to *define* what is good and true.

Again, we find explicit verification for our desire to define reality in *Planned Parenthood* v. *Casey* which states "at the heart of liberty is the right to define one's concept of existence, of meaning, of the universe, of the mystery of human life." Surely everyone is entitled to define his or her "concepts" but when these "concepts" are translated into action, the public has a right to protect others against vicious behavior issuing from those concepts. Some have the "concept" that individuals of certain races or ethnic groups are inferior and are not entitled to equal rights. Surely, they are entitled to that concept, however erroneous it may be, but they are not entitled to impose their concepts on others. Not all concepts are created equal!

We prefer our freedom over what is good

Ultimately, the modern age is shockingly anarchistic in its attitudes. Even in free societies, laws are seen to be largely unwelcome restraints on human freedom; restraints we allow simply so that great harm is not done to individuals—but the fewer restraints we have the better. We have largely lost the sense that laws can put proper restraints on human freedom and be essential to protecting human goods. We see some connection between laws and justice—but largely we prefer laws that protect our freedoms rather than laws that advance our good. For instance, although few maintain that pornography is anything other than harmful for a culture, it is generally tolerated because we prefer our freedom over what is good. After the enlightenment, the view that man is fundamentally good and that his freedom to be whatever he wants to be is his most important characteristic, became pervasive. This view was accompanied by a lack of appreciation for the transcendent, by a view of man as just a more highly developed animal. As Nietzsche taught, man ought not to control his passions by his reason, but ought to use his reason to help him to fulfill his passions; to help him to grab whatever happiness he can in this ultimately meaningless universe. This view replaced the Christian vision of man as a guest in God's universe, a creature flawed by original sin, yet God's most exalted creation, who through obedience to the laws of nature and of God and through grace, was on a journey to eternal union with God.

Sexual promiscuity increases

By the late sixties and early seventies, the view of the human person as an animal whose passions should govern became firmly entrenched in the attitudes of those who were promoting the sexual revolution. One of the greatest agents and promoters of the sexual revolution has been Planned Parenthood.[12] In the sixties and seventies many of the spokesmen and women for Planned Parenthood unashamedly advocated sex outside of marriage and even promoted promiscuity. Young people were told to abandon the repressive morals of their parents and to engage in free love. They were told that active sexual lives with a number of partners would be psychologically healthy, perfectly normal and perfectly moral. Now, largely because of the spread of AIDS and the devastations of teenage pregnancy, even Planned Parenthood puts a value on abstinence. Yet they have no confidence that young people can and will abstain from sexual intercourse, so they advocate "safe" sex, "responsible" sex, whereby they mean sexual intercourse wherein a contraceptive is used. Sex educators assume that young people will be engaging in sexual activity outside of marriage (a self-fulfilling assumption in some respects); thus the chief goal of their programs is to get them to use contraception. Planned Parenthood thinks that sex education will reduce the number of pregnancies and thus the number of abortions. But, again, all the studies show that sex education programs inspired by Planned Parenthood lead to more sexual promiscuity, more teen pregnancy and more abortion.

Young people do not need sex education of the Planned Parenthood type; they need to learn that sexual intercourse can be engaged in responsibly and safely only within marriage. Rather than filling young people's heads with false notions about freedom, and filling their wallets with condoms, we need to help them see the true meaning of human sexuality. We need to help them learn self-control and self-mastery so that they are not enslaved to their sexual passions. They need to learn that sexual intercourse belongs within marriage, and that with the commitment to marriage comes true freedom; the freedom to give of one's self completely to another, the freedom to meet one's responsibilities to one's children.

There are two cornerstones on which education for sexual responsibility should be built—cornerstones that are both corroded by contraceptive sex. One cornerstone is that sexual intercourse is meant to be the expression of a deep love for another individual, a deep love that leads one to want to give of oneself totally to another. Most individuals hope one day to be in a faithful marriage, to be in a marital relationship with someone one loves deeply and by whom one is loved deeply. One of the major components of that deep love is a promise of faithfulness, that one will give oneself sexually only to one's spouse. For many it seems odd to speak of the need to be faithful to one's spouse before marriage, but such is the case. In a sense, one should love one's spouse before one even meets him or her. One should be preparing to be a good lover, a good spouse, one's whole life. This means reserving the giving of one's self sexually until one is married—for in a sense, one's sexuality belongs to one's future spouse as much as it does to one's self. A few generations ago, it was not uncommon for young people to speak of "saving themselves" for marriage. It is a phrase scoffed at today, but one that is nonetheless indicative of a proper understanding of love, sexuality and marriage. One should prepare one's self for marriage and one should save one's self for marriage.

Much damage can be done to the self through sexual intercourse outside of marriage; many come to feel that they have been exploited and that they have exploited others; many experience great alienation and lose the ability to trust another completely. Or the sexual pleasure they are experiencing hinders their ability to get to know the true character of their sexual partner and they make bad judgments about who to marry.[13] We should try to help young people see why they should not take the easy, foolish, and self-destructive path of partaking in meaningless contraceptive sex before marriage.

Contraception severs connection between sex and babies

The other cornerstone for a sex education program should be the refrain that if you are not ready for babies, you are not ready for sexual intercourse, and you are not ready for babies until you are married. Most people want to be good parents; they want to provide for their children and give them good upbringings. Contraception attempts to sever the connection between sexual intercourse and babies; it makes us feel responsible about our sexuality while enabling us to be irresponsible. Individuals born out of wedlock have a much harder start in life; have a much harder time gaining the discipline and strength they need to be responsible adults. Single mothers have very hard lives as they struggle to meet the needs of their children and their own emotional needs as well. Those who abort their babies are often left with devastating psychological scars. The price of out of wedlock pregnancy is high.

Indeed, even within marriage, contraception is destructive; it reduces the meaning of the sexual act; again it takes out the great commitment that is written into the sexual act, the commitment that is inherent in the openness to having children with one's beloved.

Thus, it should be no surprise that unlike contraceptors, those using methods of natural family planning are highly unlikely to resort to abortion should an unplanned pregnancy occur. Some argue that couples using natural family planning are as closed to having babies as are those that use contraceptives; that they too wish to engage in "baby-free" sexual intercourse. But the crucial difference is that those using NFP are not engaging in an act whose nature they wish to thwart; they are keeping to the principles of sexual responsibility. Their sexual acts remain as open to procreation as nature permits. They are refraining from sexual intercourse when they know they may conceive and engaging in sexual intercourse when they are unable to conceive—precisely because of their desire to be responsible about child-rearing.

Those who abort generally have contracepted

One real telltale difference between contraception and natural family planning is that those who abort generally have contracepted; those who use natural family planning almost never abort. When those using Natural Family Planning get pregnant unintentionally, they fully accept the pregnancy. Generally they practice NFP not to avoid pregnancy entirely but because they would like to delay a pregnancy. They generally love children and want to have them—so although a pregnancy may be inconvenient at times, it is not disastrous. It is not insignificant that NFP is used only by those who are married; they have the mutual trust and commitment to be able to practice the method.

On the other hand, those using contraception who get pregnant unexpectedly, are generally very angry, since they did everything they could to prevent a pregnancy. Those who are unmarried do face a disaster and abortion seems like a necessity since no permanent commitment has been made between the sexual partners. Those who are married have often planned a life that is not receptive to children and are tempted to abort to sustain the child-free life they have designed. I am not, of course, saying that all those who contracept are likely to abort; I am saying that many more of those who contracept do abort than those who practice natural family planning.

Contraception takes the baby-making element out of sexual intercourse. It makes pregnancy seem like an accident of sexual intercourse rather than the natural consequence that responsible individuals ought to be prepared for. Abortion, then, becomes thinkable as the solution to an unwanted pregnancy. Contraception enables those who are not prepared to care for babies to engage in sexual intercourse; when they become pregnant, they resent the unborn child for intruding itself upon their lives and they turn to the solution of abortion. It should be no surprise that countries that are permeated by contraceptive sex, fight harder for access to abortion than they do to ensure that all babies can survive both in the womb and out. It is foolish for pro-lifers to think that they can avoid the issues of contraception and sexual irresponsibility and be successful in the fight against abortion. For, as the Supreme Court stated, abortion is "necessary" for those whose intimate relationships are based upon contraceptive sex.

[1] Mary K. Zimmerman, *Passage Through Abortion* (New York: 1977)

[2] Kristen Luker, *Taking Chances: Abortion and the Decision Not to Contracept* (Berkley: 1975)

[3] Luker, 16

[4] Luker, 32

[5] Luker, 62–63

[6] Luker, 65

[7] Luker, 68

[8] Luker, 70

[9] Luker, 71

[10] Luker, 123

[11] Luker, 83

[12] For verification of the claims here made about Planned Parenthood, see George Grant, *Grand Illusions: The Legacy of Planned Parenthood* (Brentwood, TN: Wolgemuth and Hyatt Publishers, Inc. 1988) and Robert Marshall and Charles Donovan, *Blessed are the Barren* (San Francisco, CA; Ignatius Press, 1991)

[13] For a good pastoral discussion of the evils of premarital sex, see James T. Burtchaell, *For Better or Worse*, (New Jersey: Paulist Press, 1985)

Reprinted with permission from *Homiletic & Pastoral Review*, April 1993.

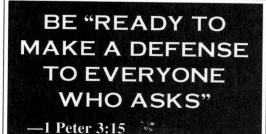